Vanishing Point

Felicity Plunkett is an award-winning and widely-published poet and critic. She has a PhD from the University of Sydney and received an Excellence in Teaching Award from the University of New England. In 2008, her manuscript *Vanishing Point* won the Thomas Shapcott Poetry Prize and was published by University of Queensland Press (UQP) the following year. Since 2010 she has been UQP's Poetry Editor. *Vanishing Point* was short-listed for the Western Australian Premier's Book Awards (Poetry), The ACT Judith Wright Prize and the Anne Elder Award.

The Arts Queensland Thomas Shapcott Poetry Prize Series

Lidija Cvetkovic *War Is Not the Season for Figs*
Jaya Savige *latecomers*
Nathan Shepherdson *Sweeping the Light Back Into the Mirror*
Angela Gardner *Parts of Speech*
Sarah Holland-Batt *Aria*
Felicity Plunkett *Vanishing Point*
Rosanna Licari *An Absence of Saints*
Vlanes *Another Babylon*
Nicholas Powell *Water Mirrors*
Rachael Briggs *Free Logic*
David Stavanger *The Special*
Krissy Kneen *Eating My Grandmother: a Grief Cycle*

WINNER OF THE 2008 THOMAS SHAPCOTT POETRY PRIZE

Felicity Plunkett
Vanishing Point

UQP

First published 2009 by University of Queensland Press
PO Box 6042, St Lucia, Queensland 4067 Australia
Reprinted 2013, 2015

www.uqp.com.au

University of Queensland Press uses papers that are natural, renewable and recyclable products made from wood grown in sustainable forests. The logging and manufacturing processes conform to the environmental regulations of the country of origin.

Typeset in 11.5/14 pt Adobe Garamond by Post Pre-press Group, Brisbane
Printed in Australia by McPherson's Printing Group

Queensland Government
Arts Queensland

Sponsored by the Queensland Office of Arts and Cultural Development

Cataloguing-in-Publication Data
National Library of Australia

Plunkett, Felicity.

Vanishing point / Felicity Plunkett.

978 0 7022 3721 8 (pbk.)

A821.4

for Benjamin Felix and Imogen Zoe

Contents

Flakes of a Dream

Journey of the Dead Man 3
The Sacrament 3
Sitting Shiva 3
Cottonwoods Screen Japan 5
The Smashing of the Glass 6
The End of History 6
The Flakes of a Dream 8
Learning the Bones 9
After the Park 11
Kindergarten 13
Flakes Shaking Free 14
Ferrying 15
Your Violent Past 16

A Flake of Your Life

Venery 25
A Flake of Your Life 26
Discipline 27
The Amnesia Inversions 28
Forgetting 28
Remembering 29
Crossed Lines 30
Sea-Margins 31
Dissolve/Eviction 32
Dissolve Shot 32

Dragging the Lake 32
Eviction 33
Restraint 34
Vivamus 36

To Break Into Flakes

A Short Knitted History of the Uterus 39
Hysteria: the displaced uterus 39
Hysterectomy: the surgically approachable uterus 40
Hysterical paroxysm 41
Hysteroscope: 'a clear view of the uterus' 42
The competent uterus 43
The knitted uterus 44
Articulate 46
Lockhart's Flakes 47
Four Chambers: A Philanderer's Manual 48
The External Examination 48
In the Cold Chamber 48
Removal 49
Closing Up and Releasing the Body 50
Soft-tissue Stitching 51
Delivery 53
Contractions 55
Bathing the Baby 56
The Negative Cutter 58
Establishing Shot 58
Cut-In 59
Continuity Editing 59
Discontinuity Editing 60
Overlapping Editing 61

Stitching the Night 62
Aubade 63
Crusts 64
Pinching Out 65
The Geometry of Vanishing 66
Undersea 68
To Break Into Flakes 69

Notes 70
Acknowledgments 71

It is time for the stone to consent to bloom.
– PAUL CELAN, ‘Corona’

Flakes of a Dream

Journey of the Dead Man

We knew the world would not be the same. A few people laughed, a few people cried, most people were silent. I remembered the line from the Hindu scripture, the Bhagavad-Gita: 'Now I am become Death, the destroyer of worlds.' I suppose we all thought that one way or another – J Robert Oppenheimer, remembering the first nuclear detonation in the New Mexico desert, July 16, 1945.

THE SACRAMENT

The world's taste
poisonous behind your teeth.
Shatter all else but hold yourself intact?
Atomic radiance
bursts onto your tongue like ridicule.
Obedient in the Jornada del Muerto desert
you take Death's name: Shiva,
auspicious one.
Bride yourself with destruction
you have made.

SITTING SHIVA

Shiva (Yiddish shive, *from Hebrew* šib'â, *seven): a seven-day period of mourning after the funeral of a first-degree relative.*

Sit silent in your loveless house:
hollow rooms you nurtured
since arrival, bloodied and aching,
newly husbanded, soles jewelled and cut.
Now, with marriage a spectre, you await

the shiva visit.
Cover the mirrors.
Build hunger alone in your yearning.
Scripture's abrasion:
you shall not prepare your own food.
On the table a cutting
advertising a home-delivered shiva tray
prophesies love's hands grown idle:
the abnegation of work that wore
your own hands into parchment
as child followed child
through the rooms and beyond.
All you made, unmade, mother
of intractable solitude.
Leave your knockless door ajar:
shiva visitors arrive in silence.
Listen. The first sound will be water
flicked from wrists and palms:
the benediction and ablution
that will carry you to where
they will speak his vanished name,
tongue the Kaddish.
Drink the consolation.
And if you are alone,
if consolation has not found you
if your atonement is inadequate, then
ha-makom yenakhem otakh.

COTTONWOODS SCREEN JAPAN

After the blast there was excitement and joy. The scientists celebrated. How could they know that the second atomic explosion, the one that would decimate cities, was just weeks away? – Nathan Gutmann

What have I conceived?
Into the vast future I watched my hands
opening, a shattering of suns.
In truth, I only said two words: 'It worked.'
My Sanskrit avatar recited nothing,
breathed Shiva into my skull.
In my loves: in physics, in desert country,
I have become an immigrant.
The rhapsodic divorces the epiphanic.
In New Mexico's German dark I writhe
in averted Semitic agony,
thinking only how to illuminate:
how to do my duty.
Though I speak with the tongues of angels,
my desert hands repulse me.
Under the cottonwoods with their breath-light seeds,
I no longer have the right to speak.
Trinity, sonnets, intuition,
the secular passions,
the compulsion towards story
made later, to assuage a line of needy verbs:
revoke my security.
Leave me, in the end, to feel
the claws like any man.

THE SMASHING OF THE GLASS

What is to give light must endure burning
– Viktor Frankel

To remind us we wed sorrow
as we celebrate the heights of joy.
To remind us of the temple's razing:
our making follows sacrilege.
To show us the shattering of self:
the way love fractures the I-and-thou.
When the diabolical comes
to feast at our table
our child in the night crib
wards it off with shadows.
Broken glass between floorboards
invisible shards on your fingers:
to shake, rub and soak ameliorates nothing.
Your shivaistic tongue soaped,
your bride-silent eyes averted:
there is no washing away.

THE END OF HISTORY

Stand in the desert, your hands
open, the shards flaking away,
and call the name of Shiva.
Omega: let there be an end to it.
Death be not proud now I am become you.

Cover me with your furious limbs
and shatter me when our eyes engage.
Remember you are dust,
and unto dust shall you return.

The Flakes of a Dream

The dream settles like fog, then disperses
until it's no longer yours.
Into the dusty parts
of heart, or imagination, or wherever
this flux and rush comes from, and wants to inhabit
it mists its way.
Feeling flakes away by day:
its nightflakes sculpt themselves
into tiny ebbing miracles.

Learning the Bones

As a young country teacher, my father studied Latin.
Its symmetry dazzling and skeleton beloved:
lines of nouns like a hand's bones *radius, trapezium, pollex*
and verbs like lamps illuminating sentences.
He sat patiently with the poets, working through the *Aeneid,*
annotations pencilled into sharp relief.
Years later, I scanned pages for anarchy:
craving an ancient voice.
Through my Catullus approximations
I heard the whisperthrill of conflict in the dark: *odi et amo*.
I opened myself to the multivalent, rereading what I loved.
Now, slow in my appreciation for order, I still prefer
the ragged and the soft:
the dative: *to, for*.
In Latin
he repeated a phrase, watching death's steady advent.
Had he traced syllables back to the words of the Latin mass,
or accepted death's poor offering
of poetry's eucharistic paper:
the wafer of someone else's words in his mouth?
I had a vision of him crying out with formal passion: *confiteor*
fleshless hands open,
stretching out to touch what fled.
One doctor at the hospice knew the language,
but she was not on shift, so what he said was lost.
The loneliness of death declaimed itself.
When I thought of him, reciting Latin, or deep in
composition, abandonment,
finality wrung itself into a knot

I could not untangle. My feelings' syntax made no sense.
My hands writhed, alive – a tangle of nervous verbs,
untranslatable, escaping catechism and parsing
until a hand stopped a hand, and they were still.

After the Park

Things fade and fail, but not the dream
– Gwen Harwood

Noon emptied the park like a death.
Vanished skies swung crying.
The last woman, lingering,
I pushed the beads of a plastic abacus:
counted my losses. At night
my dreams rolled back to taste your trace
and I sailed their upswing
woke to the jolt of their stop:
salt mornings; hope's flaking-away.
But what if it were not
too late? What if, as you turned
and left our accidental meeting –
our unrehearsed universe
pressed between pages of unwritten notes –
I called your name?
Like a leak I felt it run
beneath my skin
like heat, its seep
and speed: that dark erotic flicker
launching itself: an inkling
not to turn to dust,
to wake and breathe
summer's pulse perfumed
just as when, that summer after school,
mango, grass and eros
formed an unparsable syntax:
slippery as a transferred epithet:

my swollen skin, my ungrammatical want.
I will love you presently, he said,
not meaning *now.*
But water hot in shared rockpools
bled into my centre
the snap of elastic
on my school swimming costume, teaching
the length of my thighs
and their concaves' pulse.
And now: dreams' evidence
your secret name, my body's unrest:
the way you might turn from a bookshelf
with its grammar of forgetfulness
to hold a silence just long enough
to feel the backswing that will fracture it,
presently.

Kindergarten

Morning's drive towards learning:
my language-teaching father, my preschool
days basking plump in the seventies, surprised
at history's caftaned turn.
Mrs Tomaj from Hungary, abundant
and thin with gratitude, travelled with us.
I took the back seat. This was before
seat-belts and booster seats: once I fell out,
rolled onto a moonlit shoulder of the Harbour Bridge:
gold baby sliding along a silver ribbon, lucky.
Mrs Tomaj brought me a present every day,
exclaimed at my four-year-old beauty,
inhaling me, in a language
I did not know: basil, sorrow, perfume.
Her generosity was limitless. As we drove
she talked: her lost family, walking miles
no idea what the next town held, and *darling,*
you cannot know, please God you never know,
night-time visits, trains removing parents,
siblings, and children: did she still
have children? She seemed old, alone:
my father would know but the details
died with him. I closed my eyes to look into
the world she made in that close place with us.
I confused Hungary with hungry: all appetite,
eyes trained to see the present every morning
to see beneath its paper skin and know it.

Flakes Shaking Free

And all the time something was falling away from me, the accretion of years, flakes of it shaking free and falling with each stylised blow that I struck – John Banville, Athena

A flake can follow you
like a lost dog
while you run, taking corners too fast
to escape affection's implications.
The flake as stalker:
following while you try to evade it, or perhaps
because of that evasion
turning up where you wanted to arrive
fresh, unannounced, preceded by nothing.
It poses the question
of what you can reasonably expect, or desire.
How free it would feel to jump:
to *fall in flakes, as snow,* or let the flakes fall away.
Yet each night there you are, alone
making a silent profession of faith:
its desiccated credo moves
around your mouth like crumbs.
Your own abjection excites and nauseates you
as you raise your arm
higher, and wait
to lose yourself in gravity.

Ferrying

We traced the mountain's iced girdle
to its ankles: Newcastle's shock of beach.
You shrieked, compelled seawards,
shook shells, pressed their teeth into your palm.
Your small sandals hung from my wrist,
bars rolled down the coldening sand.
All day the thought came back,
turning like a sleeper:
all this will vanish.
With us, her feet hooked under my ribs,
your unborn sister
I would deliver into a morning
fresh with death. Later
my father's post at the freeway's end
was vacant: shared driving, standing waiting
with a book open in his hand:
these generosities too heavy
trains' roars, traffic, speed:
the trip's jolts would be unbearable.
Every journey now, he had eyes' coins
cold in his palm.
That last short segment of road
was mired, adrenaline-pitted, exhausted.
It spelt the start of driving without a compass,
of being at the front.
Cars were arranged clumsily on the road,
as though through blurred eyes,
unveiling the certainty of death in glimpses,
real and unreal as the face of an unborn child.

Your Violent Past

'Dearest friend, I am glad to be able to tell you that our theory of hysteria (reminiscence, abreaction and the like) will appear in the *Neurologisches Centralblatt* on January 1, 1893, in the form of a detailed preliminary communication' – Freud to Fleiss, 1892

I

The hysteric suffers from reminiscences,
crumbling biscuits she can almost taste.
You can't escape the past, her vision says.

Her tea grows cold as night restores its graces,
dysphoric eyes in bruise-wrapped shades of grey
hysterics, suffering reminiscences.

Sugared, buttered: the catering's still subsistence's.
The soufflé sighs, admits its disarray.
You can't escape the past, her vision says.

Where memory's scattered crumbs elude defences,
hunger finds a curatorial display.
The hysteric, suffering from reminiscences,

confronts pain's stalking hot persistences
when turmoil songs slide wretched into veins.
The hysteric suffers from reminiscences.
You can't escape the past, her vision says.

2

The shallows luke-warm on childish skin.
Shoulders pinkly sore, retaining heat,
or cold from the deeper sea: striated scarification of
underskin pearls.
The beach made safe: shark nets, umbrellas, life guards.
That summer safety vanished:
walked far along the beach
or swam to claim the horizon
then she was gone.
I thought how sirens might call to her
and understood the violence that can be done to any body.

3

Sometimes I feel mute violence everywhere.
Wherever I could hide, that's where it goes.
Violence has its ways, it has its flair:

insinuating hands trawl through my hair.
And its taste, its white and powdered haunting glow:
sometimes I feel mute. Violence, everywhere,

behind the streetscape's ever-bright despair,
inside houses, in gardens' rootless grow.
Violence has its ways, and prompts despair

to reach for things my hands would never dare,
fucking up my life: a quid pro quo.
Sometimes I feel mute violence everywhere.

I search in you for a pulse of pastoral care,
some way into your book of common prayer:
sometimes I feel mute violence everywhere,
violence, with its ways, its glowing flair.

4

Violence dreams its way into your dough.
It stops the rise, deflates the swell of night,
tries fucking up your life: a quid pro quo

for all the times you tried to stop its flow
and hungered for some sweet and soft delight,
but violence dreamed its way into your dough.

Define a deal: let it bequeath its slow
and anxious fortitude, so that it might
stop fucking up your life, its quid pro quo

a promise to remember. Still, you know,
you can't recall its rationale, not quite,
as violence dreams its way into your dough.

You don't know, any more, what to bestow.
Gone now: all that you imagine could be bright,
when violence dreams its way into your dough,
starts fucking up your life, a quid pro quo.

5

Memory and memorial – the metaphors: the house,
the dig, the flow.
Freud with his fine brushes at the sites –
then later, something more circular:
back and back we go to the unmapped heart.
And hysteria: bodily remembrance of all and nothing
in its aches, emissions and admissions.
I stay in bed because the streets are running
with the loose aggression of the world we make –
its bruises deepening with the hours.

6

Morning's beach flat with heat.
Water-deafened I still hear sirens.
Shards, then: memory's filaments:
sounds, angles, tastes.
A single vision or story
forms then dissipates
until trauma is invisible
injected by each clue into agony
felt and arterial.
The water's feet, playful on my shoulder;
on my neck: a murderous conclusion
to what's been said.

7

My summer birthday gone the way
of tidewood, flooded castles.
A currentline of wanted babies
horizon-bound
where my future is rebirth. Once I lived
with pain around the edges,
wrecking sandshapes, making me
liminal, ineligible, temporary
as blown seedlings taking root:
eyes closed against the rapturous
violence of that fire.

A Flake of Your Life

Venery

Whoso list to hunt, I know where is an hind – Thomas Wyatt

You slip away. I raise my crop and fly
the moon-boned strait, this sudden gate and sweat-
flanked crest; this stretch of disappointed sky.
Suspended in your absence, blooded, hooked,
my ankles' clank disturbs the night's slow pulse.
You love me, more, perhaps, than I love you,
and yet you take the deer's part every time,
leaving me these boots, this gun, my jealous chafing
thighs, my trying not to give the game away, but then
this small boxed heart I brought you here tonight
is fresh and iced, and makes me think of days
when I wore fox-fur, smiled my shot-glass smile

and lord! I had no time for men like you,
of whom, I find, there is a dearth, alas.

A Flake of Your Life

Contemplate a flake upon you
(fallen or flown,
from *flacox*: flying, said of arrows)
and lie awake conjugating yourself.
Clear now?
Everything will blur after sunrise.
Feel the tilt of the world, feel longing
like something you can lean into
the way you did as a child
in a hot classroom.
Stare until your focus softens
into everything slow and private,
the warp and weft loosening, releasing sureness.
Flakes adhere to and fall from
the broken, chipped and crazed in you.
In flakes you glimpse a future,
or some other time, ghosted with imaginings:
what we slough off unaware
might become, for someone else, precious and troubling.
The moon's face removes itself
behind clouds' purdah,
the way you must move, ethical,
with what has lodged, and what is to come,
fabricated into glitter.

Discipline

John Banville, the fifth Beatle, pesto, cake
(or friand) – anyway, we talked. And
when we didn't, days felt long. John Banville
with his longer oeuvre my compensation:
burnt CDs; unknotting reef and clove knot,
rolling hitch: the verbal boy-scoutery
of your ever-casual emails: these and when
not these, the things we'd said: the glance you gave,
the way you leant back in the lift one day
and with that, all my floor leant into you
and I was thrown, my skinned knees anchors:

Oh stupid girl! How much of this could be
misprision, missed points, mise-en-scène?
But missing, with its sighs and crumbs, drags on.

The Amnesia Inversions

FORGETTING

I give you back the dreams you start in me.
I set off, fast, from where I set you down.
Forgetting gets me past the place I see

your knees, your flakes, your curiosity
your syncopated heart, that fleeting frown –
I give you back the dreams you start in me.

The way amnesia works: steps one to three:
with every cell ablaze, your heart unsewn,
forgetting. Get me past the place I see.

First, count them, kiss them, trace the filigree
of nascent strokings underneath my gown.
I give you back the dreams you start in me

of how your dark warms people lost at sea
or anyway, the landscapes of your heart's renown:
I give you back the dreams you start in me
forgetting (very soon) the place I see.

REMEMBERING

I take you through the contours of my day:
the way words press your hands into my night,
my flooded outskirts' almost-disarray

those thoughtful sighs do nothing to allay.
I press soft petals down into the light
and take you through the contours of my day.

Within my acanthine communiqué
your wading boots tread hard on my contrite
and flooded outskirts, almost. Disarray

is something you can overplay
like rocky road, or gardener's delight.
I take you through. The contours of your day:

you watch your hands, you whip up a soufflé
then write three poems, and glancingly invite
my flooded outskirts' almost-disarray

with everything and nothing. And your prey
and predator join hands, their wedding night
will take you through the contours of our day,
my flooded outskirts' almost-disarray.

Crossed Lines

We descend the mountain like mist.
Road twists plot
the tired screenplay of our mutual life.
You asked me to ventriloquise Doris Day.
We played pillow talk,
until, jack of the blond wig,
I veered off into dark counterpoint.
We fed each other lines on the trip up here.
We'd have a house, a fence, a baby seat in the car.
How much your secret ripped my equilibrium
you'll never ask. Your mirror-fixed eyes
see you smile at your future. Your pack of lies
fell on the table with a flat clean slap,
clapping the newborn bottom of your universe. You
took the loose threads of my costume
and ravelled backwards.
We drive down now. I wear magnanimity's bandage
and wonder whether
I'll ever not fake it again.

Sea-Margins

In shells' curled ears the sea's lost memory sleeps.
I long to taste its salt across my tongue.
My drying thighs forget its salty deeps.

All night the mountain works its iron lung:
adenoidal, wheezing, thirsty for the damp.
I long to taste sea's salt across my tongue.

Desire under my hands, desire a cramp
whose rhythms wake remembering's fitful doze:
adenoidal, wheezing, thirsty for the damp.

Trace soft inscriptions of what skin can disclose,
touching the ancient prints of urgings' scars
whose rhythms wake remembering's slow doze.

Of all my waking selves, my avatars,
here resides the slow protean power most
touching. The ancient prints of urgings' scars

rise humming: I listen for the place, where,
in shells' curled ears, the sea's lost memory sleeps
entwined with coral, brine and water's glare.
My drying thighs forget its salty deeps.

Dissolve/Eviction

DISSOLVE SHOT

salt water: applied to wounds
a guarantee of closure
it might sting, but if you're smart
you'll do it anyway
infection can't burgeon
unfurling itself in your veins
stopped like some pillar, some lover
the body lost in salt

salt water: appears subject to transformation
parches the attempting tongue
breeds salt, factory of the lachrymose
but the sea is bigger than that, impervious
escape has a charge, she can't afford it –
her small grief turnstiled by the sea

DRAGGING THE LAKE

trawling: something left behind
checking locks at night

unravelling like etymology, knitted girl

the lake's bed
velutinous, swaying with erotic intent

EVICTION

old love letters block *chi*
the portmanteau prohibitive

in the end why keep broken promises
if not to cut at hope

in boxed photos
she finds self-effacement
apparitions of girls and women
plaited into biography's mythic cords

through the maze of inner city without
prophesying speed bumps, dead ends
chicanery's pleasures

the dream ripens
into a bodysong
her right foot is sure and heavy

Restraint

Soft now on their wooden clavicles
each of your frocks once knew its place.
When you kneeled over green shoots
probing the places where basil starts;
poured cups of tea for patients who waited
on your veranda, for your husband, the doctor;
when you walked three miles to town
with warm scones, silver beet
or a piece of your mind
or stooped in the crotchety dusk
writing to your granddaughters:
your frock always said what it needed to, no more.
Now I run my hands through
mended cotton, starched linen
stiff skirts, blouses still holding a remembered body
and my touch awakens mothball mint and lavender –
those ghostly scents.
Which one dazzled you, a young bride brought
to this small town by your new husband:
passionate, scholarly, mercurial, handing you joy and grief
from his pockets, as if you were a child, and these his gifts?
Which did you wear home from hospital
your dead baby swaddled with
self-loathing and rage?
Which for the days when your three babies
made and remade you?
Or when you set out alone, a widow,
travelling into a new life

leaving a marriage carefully mended,
hand-washed with frugal pleasure
darned to outlast the summers that faded it?

Vivamus

Kiss me, he says. I can't see through your knee
she says. They laugh, he shifts. They watch the night
unfolding into glassy blades of light.
The news behind his thighs is rolling blue:
it semaphores a bruised and anxious world
of which they are no longer much a part.
Violence comes up to darken love-warm skin,
purples into flower, drops its sallow head:
what happens to old aches our fingers
press for but find vanished? What if history's
dissolution passes through our bodied
moments traceless, as it passes through parts
it once lit up: abandoned, hauntless, harmless
now: with sorrow loosened; every cell renewed.

To Break Into Flakes

A Short Knitted History of the Uterus

HYSTERIA: THE DISPLACED UTERUS

Hippocrates coins the term
in the fourth century BC
imagining the womb as wanderer, displaced,
searching for children.
Picture this father of medicine
grey head gravid
melancholy with the ache of lost babies.
In the second century
Aretaeus of Cappadocia, his disciple,
teaches that the uterus
'much like an independent animal'
makes its migrations around the body
towards the fragrant.
Treatment for this maundering
(with its concomitant choking,
crushing of other organs
and heaviness of the head)
involves smoothing perfume
around the lower orifices
to persuade the uterus back
from its nomadic elusions.

Imagine this pear, this organ:
strange and melancholy
the itinerant uterus
moved like Eve by desire:
tracking the body, longing
for a child from within itself

to know the scent of a newborn skull.
It trawls the night
inhaling the dark's swollen scents
the way desire moves
restlessly, towards, towards.

HYSTERECTOMY: THE SURGICALLY APPROACHABLE UTERUS

The nineteenth century discovers
Dr James Blundell,
inventing blood transfusions,
creating and naming instruments
for that purpose:
the Impellor, the Gravitator.
Despite asserting that the abdomen is
'surgically approachable'
in *The Principles and Practice of Obstetricy*,
he warns against intervention
in birthing, allowing breach-positioned babies
to shift and flip, to orient
their advent with idiosyncratic grace,
discovering their blood's rhythm.
Employing forceps with caution, less often
than his peers, he performs the first
successful caesarean-hysterectomy
in London, 1828, radically
cutting out a womb and foetus
to save mother and child.
The blades of hospital administration
reflect him severely.
He resigns, slips bruiselessly from the vein

to pursue private practice,
reads insatiably and travels
between expectant patients,
later retiring to focus
on a passion for the classics.

Think of him:
outstretched hands
measuring reverence
visionary possibility
balanced with confidence
in birth's ancient knowledge
and all this expelled:
eclipsed by the cantering
'cascade of intervention'
with its barbaric face
its occlusions and excisions.
Think of him,
defeated, unpraised in his lamp-lit carriage,
basking in the fragrance
of the pages
he escapes to,
and wish for him consolation, joy.

HYSTERICAL PAROXYSM

While Blundell reads his way
into the nineteenth century,
an eruption of hysteria
(afflicting two-thirds of women
and characterised by
a tendency to cause trouble)

ushers into vogue a treatment:
'inducing paroxysm'
in women patients.
The treatment, though not new,
is suddenly ubiquitous and
with it comes
the invention of the vibrator,
a labour-saving medical device
for the midwives and physicians
who administer the treatment.
This respectable remedy
is widely advertised, for example,
in needlepoint magazines.
In 1952 the American Psychiatric Association
discontinues use of the term 'hysteria'
(now see
Histrionic Personality Disorder)
and with that,
the vibrator goes underground.

HYSTEROSCOPE: 'A CLEAR VIEW OF THE UTERUS'

Hysteroscope, speculum, colposcope
collaborate to uncover a clear view
of cervix and uterus.
This battery of scopic objects
ushers in bad prospects:
problems *in situ*
and Latinate explanations.
Microscopic hooks grip
the folds of her lips.
Conisation re-sculpts the cervix

light-cutting away tissue.
If she presses up hard against luck
the margins will exceed the lesion.
Side effects may include
a weakening
of the cervix.
A doctor tells her:
Your cervix may be incompetent.
(Where is your cells' diligence: muscles, body
obedient to the last corpuscle?)
Scarring makes conception difficult
or delivery uncertain, if the foetus holds.
In other words, she is told,
as her competent surgeon shuts her file
her smile confected within its margins:
Your cervix may not now do
any of the things a cervix should.
But if we need it,
we still have hysterectomy
as an option
to keep ahead of the cancer.

THE COMPETENT UTERUS

Thou hast knitted me together
in my mother's womb – Psalm 139

What goes on in the dark?
You form yourself, pearl one,
or you are formed,
as though stitch by stitch,

row by row.
The pattern's next coded line
fabricates itself.
All the yearning and knowing
that goes before the needlework:
you were there, where?
You rolled the soft ball of yourself
down the corridors
of my interrupted dreaming
before the knitting began
in and through
not by me, no –
through you I am becoming,
and you are,
and this is the greatest yes.

THE KNITTED UTERUS

2004 and a bright pink woollen uterus appears to dance
on the keys of an old piano
then swing from a tree.
In a third photo,
fallopian tubes are arms
flexed as the womb assumes a pose.
The anatomy student who created the uterus
for an online knitting site
describes it as
a 'cute cuddly knitted uterus doll'
but notes: 'it's not completely anatomically correct'
and 'of course, the human uterus
is not bubblegum pink.'

And though the womb, of course,
is neither pink, nor a climber of trees,
it dances, and is more than the sum of its cells.

Articulate

An elephant's face emerged between his palms
its whimsical felt ears fell away
but driftwood bodied-forth articulated vertebrae
and limbs that moved in ripples until, voiced with age
they careened towards oil in the rhythm of their soughing.
Wood-skin baked grey after drowning
burnished at its rolling haunches,
remembers his corrugated hands.
He must have sanded alone at night
a line of bogong moths under an oil lamp,
the scrap of a cigarette forgotten at the side of his smile,
until each curve invited and repaid stroking:
your father who came late and humble to love
from the dry-dock of habitual pleasure
when your mother's flinching solitude
softened, pain sharpening her bones.
When he wound his wrists into her curls,
his fire flared and singed his netted fingers.
He made this toy the way he made you –
the son who survived it all –
from nothing more than hope
from whatever, in the end, was to hand
when he looked to the coast
receding from the small conjugal vessel
he had fashioned and set afloat
on these late gilded joists, his radial creation.

Lockhart's Flakes

Wherever there is contact between two objects there is a transfer of material between them. Forensic scientists must find that material and discover where it originated from – The Lockhart Principle

A flake of paint from her doorframe
in the car of the fleeing felon
'provides very strong evidence
that the suspect was at the scene':
the flake gives of itself, it is something
that *has been or become detached from*
some other life.
The detective explains to the woman
how the smallest traces of DNA can be found:
how crimes have signatures whose flakes we can read
how 'it is certain we will nail the perpetrator',
warming to the subject, to the benefits of progress,
to science, with its cold juridical eye,
as she holds her cardigan tighter,
everything unflaking, lost,
whatever, whoever may be found.

Four Chambers: A Philanderer's Manual

THE EXTERNAL EXAMINATION

Calculate the weight
of breasts, wrists, intentions
with the scales of your autopsic eye.
Make your observations of clothing and its position.
Run through a general description of the body,
salient features only. For example:
well-nourished female, medium height,
around thirty,
rounded thighs, hairless legs.
Save your false compare
your *skin like alabaster, perfect breasts*
your *sunlight nimble in her hair.*
Do not delve into the slab of light
across her eyes.
Softness will not assist
your peregrinations –
the maps you move by
are the much-handled ones
you hold and fold over years.
Keep the language simple:
all you desire is the anatomy
correct, just as you expect.

IN THE COLD CHAMBER

Be meticulous about self-covering.
Protect your skin. Gloves' meniscus
holds your truth aloof.

Observe scrupulously
the protocols of containment.
Sharply scissor the sartorial ensemble
she proffers artlessly.
Disambiguate. Tell her
the one about your wrecked heart
and acquisitive ex-wife,
your penchant for forgetfulness
and hunger for diversity.
Make it sound like equity, nature, honesty.
Keep expectation's flame low.
Force hope's head down
over torturing waters until she relents,
consents: demands no more than pleasure
pure in the instant, string- and sting-less:
the polite pornography that restrains
obscenity: avert your gaze, keep back
the pericardial sac with its hold on
bruised treasure
the embrace of the arterial.

REMOVAL

Concentrate your gaze upon her
feel your bulimic appetite rise
with your passion for metrology:
how each body is alike,
and with your eyes closed,
you can make her anyone you like.
Rokitansky or Virchow:
it doesn't matter which pathologist's manual
you follow. Either way, things can be neat,

an exemplar of meticulousness.
Move down the body,
longitudinal, methodical.
Remove and isolate
cerebellum and cerebrum:
brain-cutting is less effort than you expect.
Sluice the fluids of tenderness.
All your fears fruit
when the body's stillness offers itself
to something like cadaveric spasm.

CLOSING UP AND RELEASING THE BODY

Let disposability assist you like a diener.
So much can be bagged up these days,
you say, cigarette lingering
at your mouth's turned corner,
the afterwards chat more delightful
than the mined advent path.
Envisage your restraint:
your calm performance:
the legendary prosector
strolling the body's streets
in his dinner suit –
a meticulous procession to dinner,
the opera, the provenance of his vital wife,
his erstwhile and overarching existence.
Do not pause in the doorway.
Head home, head back, swim powerfully forward
in the vast purgation that comes
to wash your memory,
to excise delinquency.

Soft-tissue Stitching

Through the pink pelvis a rubber doll
descends into an overheated room.
Breathless, we await her first breath.
A woman with a small mouth rips the silence:
Does Hubby have to look at the business end
while it comes out?
We have embarked on the tour.
        These reliquary spaces
        will absorb our privacy.
        We will leave it here
        swaddled, abandoned
        awaiting
                its quiet case, its glassed future.
In a merry disguising tone,
with a gleam in her curatorial eye,
the midwife says:
Our birthing suites were converted from an old storage room.
A cupboard swings open.
Inside everything clicks,
shiny as a stretched perineum.
Concealed here are instruments to compel birth
laid out with steely logic as a riposte
        to the beautiful unruliness of labia, blood
        and our reasons for being here.
These are the objects we have fashioned
to hurry life, to make it fit our measures,
to start the breath, if that is needed.
And, at the end, when the last of life is removed,
when the wards are theatre-dark,

they will recede with metallic bodies
into secret places.
The men, as if on a school excursion, are invited
to take turns inhaling gas and air:
to keep them interested and distracted,
stitched back into what is unbroken.

Delivery

transferred
whole onto this shore by waves, so that erosion
is its very face – Jorie Graham

I remember her flat belly,
her concave hips,
and the smooth skin between them.
I remember the taut silk of her conversation,
the way she had
of stirring up an afternoon, her head
full of solitude and metaphor,
all her angular longings and ambitions,
scars' absence and how that absence lied about the invisible.

I thought about all she didn't know yet
and I was drenched with jealousy, sadness, desire for her
innocence.
I liked her more as I grew away from her,
and murderously I knew
every inch of that sweet skin, that flat heart.
She had a way of standing at the threshold,
leaning into doorframes, watching me:
eyes all elegy, but bright with a shared, secret glee.
She knew what it meant to want something so much
that the night spread out in cold sheets,
trying to unlearn a love she'd imagined or misunderstood,
trying to forget the lie she had warmed herself against,
always knowing it was a lie.

She didn't know what I'd do or had done
to her. I ached for her to come with me always:
her irresistible eyes. Already I was swooning with new,
but it comforted me not to lose her.
I held her hand beyond the allocated time
for new arrivals.

I plaited my fingers around her throat
and released a song she would drown in.
I called her into my fresh fecundity,
wanting to remember girlish breasts with their pink nipples.
At the edge of the room, out of the world's line of sight
we would smoulder quietly under the cover of maternity.
It was meant to be her death
but together
we dreamed our way beyond it.

Later, she would whisper to me of everything your birth
would silence:
her pristine days and wild nights, the afternoons
languid with sorrow, sleepless pleasure –
my ruptured doze its sideshow-mirrored twin.
That rush to meet, the restless waiting,
appetite gone, lost somewhere in feeling,
all this your newness, and my bliss, resembled.

I trembled with her death
shimmering in its rush and flood
that all my body fought, and fought towards.
I felt emerge the skull of triumph's
solitary yell.

My body broke open like a laugh.

Contractions

Are they rolling me out of the room
on a gurney, the body bag laid open,
my breast stitched, heart removed, weighed, assessed?

Has life been lifted out of me:
metal cap on flexible skullplates?

While they bent to regard epiphanic eyes
I was alone with my knees pulled up, shuddering,
waiting to be stitched up, as though this had yet to happen.

Bathing the Baby

the baby's body is slippery
in the bath
the woman's panicking hands
clasp and reclasp
her fingers circling newborn arms
firm and certain
like monkey bars
the woman is swinging from the baby
the baby's head nods
she suffers no confusion
the woman feels anxiety
slipping over her mouth like a hand
someone larger is holding her up
it would be easier
to let the baby swim alone
in her pram with the cicada wheels
the baby promenades
the woman can't stop the wheels' pull
dragging behind she leans back
away from the hurtling pram
all her energy thin
against the baby's recklessness
this dare-devil baby
lies quiet at night
learning the room's face
eyes dropping shut against the woman's privacy
clicking open like a doll's
the baby is a neat clerk
in a cardigan

monitoring, detached, observant
the baby jumps trains in the dark
the pull of the baby is deafening
the baby sings underwater

The Negative Cutter

ESTABLISHING SHOT

A shot, usually involving a distant framing, that shows the spatial relations among the important figures, objects and setting in a scene.

The doctor hands you a splinter.
You hold it carefully, then wrap and tend it –
you wake at night to its small wails, its relentless hunger.
Returning to the surgery to see 'the films',
in which hidden parts of your body star
you find yourself onscreen,
as dissolution into dark and light.
Past that vain impulse to preen,
you lurch to self-critical disgust, spotted with denial.
The doctor notes the salient features,
you're his pupil, and you star, destined to outgrow him.
He clears his throat in a genteel sort of way
that suggests nothing more than a schooling in tact.
He asks your permission to show the film,
but is shy with you. Your resplendence dazzles.
Like your friends, children and colleagues,
he speaks to you in a careful voice, new, respectful:
mindful of the insouciance
and trouble you are cultivating within.

CUT-IN

An instantaneous shift from a distant framing to a closer view of some portion of the same space.

The splicing is easy. There are tools for cutting negatives.
Words have the precision of surgery, and the practice:
excision's clean edges. No room for doubt or faithless nights.
A series of scrubbed professionals wax: how positive they are.
We make one incision. Pop in and nip it out.
Your face assumes a picture book benignity.
Reassurance pours on you, treacly,
and your bitterness occludes.
The moon is bitten to bleeding.
The nights linger on like guests who don't take the hint,
sullen-coloured, lit with an illusory pre-dawn glow.
You watch the days start up like coughing cars.

CONTINUITY EDITING

A system of cutting to maintain continuous and clear narrative action.

Through the stages of grieving like a gymkhana pony.
Call action. You are strong and blithe.
This is the 'cheat cut'. Everything looks the same,
though technically it's not.
The sun rolls up where yesterday's did,
and if there was a tree, a gnarled grudge,
or someone's worry beads,
they're there too. The props department has been at work,
while the editors have been dreaming,

the director nonchalant.
There are accolades: you have *come through*.
You are *not making a fuss*, you are *keeping it together*.
In a caravan before your face is prepared
your handkerchief twists, your eyes are bloodshot.
Nights are drenched in the music of remembrance.
You learn the script, but your voice is distant.
Only close inspection would discover
your days don't match:
the illusion of the continuous.

DISCONTINUITY EDITING

Any alternative system of joining shots together using techniques unacceptable within *continuity editing* principles. Possibilities would include mismatching of temporal and spatial relations, violations of the *axis of action*, and concentration on graphic relationships.

Clowns rehearse outside the next caravan.
You crush words hard against your teeth.
They fly out of your mouth like shots
or you spit them, blooded and cutting,
fretted and strung with beads of shiny feeling.
You are drowning inside yourself, alone.
Anger jerks out of you, or unstopped crying that falls fluent
the way it does in dreams: salty, benedictory.
The skirt of your feelings, stuck in the car door,
flaps at passersby without your knowing.

OVERLAPPING EDITING

Cuts that repeat part or all of an action.

A letter from a dead man
is remarkable. In the dream I knew I should keep it.
As it dissolved in my hands, I forgot your words:
vanishing evidence of an after-death conversation.
My fingers sieved sand.
I couldn't hold the letter-grains:
our correspondence of air.

Stitching the Night

Night's stitches, black along the sky's hem
dissolve into a slow drip of morning birdsong
that picks at your veins, accelerates and is complex
as the fingers of a seamstress,
the intricate gestures of a conductor's wrists.
You close your eyes and trace
harmonies of point and counterpoint
into the gordian school of mourning
where you have enrolled; chosen
death as your special subject, your major
arcana: radial, bridal, electrifying.
Morphine's steady eye regards you
as you find and relinquish last generosities:
your first pay's fruit, the gold pocket watch
to gild a grandson,
the wooden elephant your father crafted
for my unborn child, the evasive face
whose burgeoning you celebrate
though its prolepsis shows you
vitality's amnesia, its infidelity.
Still, now, you find in mobility
something that opens in your face –
a poise before graduation, delight
in the onward sewing, in what can be made
from a fabric in its afterlife

Aubade

The breakfast trolley makes a single cut
and morning's door flies open
metallically shattering the small sleep my stitches pick at.
Outside the roll of hills is violet-soft, colostrum-hued.

I lie awake still working on the toe-and-finger count.
Your eyes regard me skeptically under the rise and fall
of downed fontanelle:
your nectarine breath pours down my chin.

Goodnight, my love, at five, when sunrise
probes your radiant sleep.
The mynahs' whines' steady drip feeds my veins' ache:
and yet what dark skies we saw, my ceiling-smashing girl.

Crusts

The mynahs go to school
on your refused crusts.
The blinds imitate
what your brother calls
the flap-flap-wait of wings.
Another storm siren
flirts its purple way
across an unresponsive sky.
You fly into sleep.

I lie on the white bed
heat climbing my thighs
as morning's skirts
fall away.
I feel the weight of my hands'
emptiness.

You have returned my breasts to me
with a handful of pats
and the wise spare language
you prefer:
the gentlest of removals.
You place your hand
inside my singlet
your cheek under my clavicle
before your doll's eyes click shut.

Pinching Out

When new growth starts, 'tip pruning' or 'pinching out' may be necessary to encourage further branching – Yates Garden Guide

The garden's slant afternoon eye halves her.
A shadow hangs long from her feet:
growing downwards – rooted, celled,
going awry, multiplying furiously, inhabiting the dark.
Fingers at her soles, stroking the hollows:
the weight of denial fills her belly.

She is a small pocket filled with all things lost:
an envelope shaken from a book, phrased with
the memory of words for pain, stones collected
on some walk in the before, some benign occasion.

You can cut a pelargonium to light its fuse again,
footless limbs in compost, accepting illusion for the known,
a lover's face in the blade, making life in her:
her ankles shallow; the green surge thrumming within.

The Geometry of Vanishing

Ultimate cliff where all lines converge
to fall away to their burial,
impossible to envisage or exhume:
vanishing point, a comfort invented
to tame the end, to tidy stories' geometry.
I practised a kind of lovemaking,
jerry-built a honeycomb home
sow's-ear low-ceilinged fabrication
like my grandparents in the Depression:
mute and frugal, using whatever was to hand,
desire rolled like a swag,
bundled small and tight
expectancy corseted: breathing in, hook
and eye, I blew
the hourglass that housed
my own suffocation,
tried to exude an absent sun
from between my palms:
to warm the earth into imagination.
I thought of the farmer I met
on the cliff-edged mountain road
shooting the collapsed kangaroo,
vanishing its skewed-limbed agony:
a violence of kindness.
I found nothing to know in this garden:
mothering instead a messy intersection
where bricks, glass and sand would break
down into their particles.
I could not make my children wait

crumbless and unmothered
night-crying in my sweet-forested absence.
I set out to face down the end:
to feel disaster's sharp
point under my sole;
its bite poisonous like the prick
of a spider when I was pregnant.
Its venom, the posturing Austrian doctor,
scenting my blood and flowering, hostile,
told me, would not cross – not everything
crosses – the placenta.
Not everything shapes the mobile skull.
My feet met the water's cold shoulder.
So close to finality I had to
feel a way with my fingertips,
carrying on my back the atlas
of disappointment and two cuttings.
I found at the edge of the world
an unimagined curve:
not the papercuts of hostile scripture
nor a scorched skull with eyeholes
to thread my fingers through
and feel a final blindness: eyeless myself
in the pocked face of decimation's strait.
Instead, I found my feet in a cradle.
Cells fidgeted and shaped themselves:
a factory of lines, alive, industrious:
moving out to start new stories
the generation of everything:
the blood's start.

Undersea

Waterblind beneath verdancy.
Your fingers crochet small repairs in me
where softness exquisitely frays:
inside your seaplant-smooth top lip
I find enbrailled letter-spores
that describe ways into the heart,
but letters lean awry, words
waver and fall apart
forming wordlessness:
fabric's doing undone:
sometimes the clearest vision is
of etymology's release:
the possibility of re-imagining.
Where the buried ferry sleeps
we traced the harbour's belly,
between the moored and mobile
deep into the unfathomable
so that our limbs could ribbon,
foreknowing their unravelling:
bodies overturned, rolling, the polite thou-and-I
making its mouth-first way into the conjoined,
approximating birth:
love's vernix whitens two swimmers
against the cold before
the depths disgorge them,
blood-gas fizzing,
finding ways of breathing again: new ways.

To Break Into Flakes

To peel off or separate in flakes. To fall in flakes, as snow. To remove in flakes. To break flakes or chips from; break into flakes; to flake fish for a casserole. To cover with or as if with flakes. To form into flakes
– Random House Dictionary

And when you pin and catch feeling in words
the tissue of its inconstancy
flakes away in your hands.
You push flakes into shapes and call this reality
and smear nouns' concrete between its parts
until you have something you can believe and live in.
But on those days when past and future jumble
you think maybe everything is aflake
soft and tentative, and only ever temporary:
the quiet fall at night outside your window
beckons you forever back, forwards, into.

Notes

'Journey of the Dead Man': This poem juxtaposes the Hindu god Shiva, as invoked by Oppenheimer, with the idea of sitting shiva, the Jewish mourning ritual, to explore kinds of creativity and destruction and their connections. In 'Sitting Shiva', *ha-makom yenakhem otakh* is a Hebrew blessing, spoken at the end of the shiva visit: 'May God comfort you', in the form addressed to a woman alone.

'Your Violent Past': the title comes from Low's 'Drums and Guns'. The article by Freud and Fleiss contains the line: 'Hysterics suffer mainly from reminiscences'.

'A Flake of Your Life' takes its title from Leonard Cohen's 'Famous Blue Raincoat'.

'*Vivamus*': the title is borrowed from Catullus' Poem 5 which starts '*Vivamus mea Lesbia atque amemus*' ('Let us live, my Lesbia, and let us love', or, simply, 'Let's live').

'Four Chambers': Rokitansky and Virchow, mentioned in 'Removal', are considered the giants of pathology, and each physician had a distinctive method of autopsic examination.

'False compare' is from Shakespeare's sonnet 130.

'The Negative Cutter: An Introduction to Editing' : all epigraphs are from David Bordwell and Kristin Thompson, *Film Art: An Introduction*, 6th edition, (New York: McGraw-Hill, 2001).

Acknowledgments

I am grateful for an Emerging Writer's Grant from the Literature Board of the Australia Council in 2005 and for Dorothy Sargent Rosenberg prizes in 2006 and 2007, awarded for a number of poems in this manuscript.

In 2000 I benefited from a mentorship with Dorothy Porter at The Writers' House, Varuna. Dorothy was an inspiring and generous mentor, crucial to the development of my writing.

I would like to thank the editors of *Best Australian Poetry 2008*, *The Best Australian Poems 2008*, *Heat*, *Blue Dog*, *Calyx: Thirty Contemporary Australian Poets* (Paper Bark Press), *The Literary Review: Australian Poetry Sampler* and *JIGS: Journal of Interdisciplinary Gender Studies*, in which a number of the poems in this manuscript first appeared, in earlier forms. Thank you to The Red Room Company who commissioned 'The Negative Cutter: An Introduction to Editing' for the Poetry Picture Show.

Thanks to Anthony Lawrence for his generous intuition and ruthless advice and to Bronwyn Lea for her acute suggestions and vision. Wendy James and John Turner have been my first readers, whose enthusiasm and creativity have enriched this work.

Thanks to my friends and family for encouragement and practical support, especially Diana Plunkett, Madeleine Lawrence, Yasmin Haskell, Jude Seaboyer, Amanda

O'Callaghan, Ruth Blair, Margaret Gibson, Matthew Karpin, Ann Hamer, David Hamer, Anne Grimes Alice Bechtel and William Simon. Thanks, too, to my students at the University of Queensland for inspiration.